The brown marmorated stink bug is one of five thousand stink bug species around the world. It will eat almost anything. It sticks its *proboscis* (feeding tube) into a wide variety of trees and many types of fruits, vegetables, row crops, nuts, and other plants. Farmers lose millions of dollars every year to damage caused by stink bugs. They are especially difficult to kill as stink bugs can be resistant to many common pesticides.

Stink bugs have scent glands that emit their unpleasant odor. This smell is mostly used as a defense mechanism to prevent other animals from eating them. The stink-bug smell is also used for mating and as an aggregation smell, or a smell telling other stink bugs where to go. People think stink bugs smell like coriander, filthy socks, rotten fruit, or cilantro.

But everyone agrees—stink bugs smell BAD!

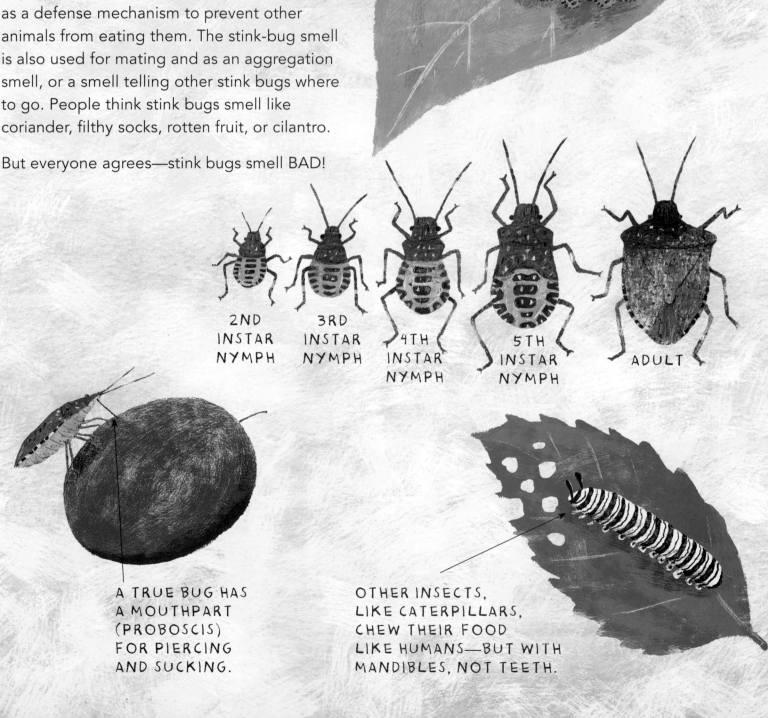

2ND INSTAR NYMPH

3RD INSTAR NYMPH

4TH INSTAR NYMPH

5TH INSTAR NYMPH

ADULT

A TRUE BUG HAS A MOUTHPART (PROBOSCIS) FOR PIERCING AND SUCKING.

OTHER INSECTS, LIKE CATERPILLARS, CHEW THEIR FOOD LIKE HUMANS—BUT WITH MANDIBLES, NOT TEETH.

AAS (American Association for the Advancement of Science)/Subaru Excellence in Children's Books Finalist

Cooperative Children's Book Center Best Book of the Year List

Science magazine's Best Books for Curious Kids

Virginia Readers' Choices

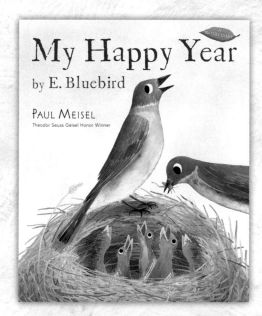

A Junior Library Guild Selection

"A brief, friendly journal-style text accompanied by equally uncluttered and appealing digitally enhanced paintings in sumptuous colors." —*Horn Book*

MY STINKY SUMMER

····· BY S. BUG ·····

PAUL MEISEL

HOLIDAY HOUSE · NEW YORK

For organic farmers. And for everyone who's
had an experience with stink bugs and thought,
Ew. Stink bug!

Special thanks to Louis N. Sorkin, B.C.E., American Museum of National History

HOLIDAY HOUSE is registered in the U.S. Patent and Trademark Office.
Printed and bound in February 2020 at Toppan Leefung, Dong Guan City, China.
The artwork was created with watercolors, acrylics, and digital tools.
www.holidayhouse.com
First Edition
1 3 5 7 9 10 8 6 4 2

Library of Congress Cataloging-in-Publication Data

Names: Meisel, Paul, author.
Title: My stinky summer by S. Bug / Paul Meisel.
Description: First edition. | New York : Holiday House, [2020]
Series: A nature diary ; 3 | Audience: Ages 4–8 | Audience: Grades K–1
Summary: "Told in diary form, My Stinky Summer by S. Bug introduces
readers to the stinkbug's life cycle and survival habits"—Provided by publisher.
Identifiers: LCCN 2019045792 | ISBN 9780823440535 (hardcover)
ISBN 9780823448197 (epub)
Subjects: LCSH: Stinkbugs—Juvenile literature.
Classification: LCC SB945.P47 M45 2020 | DDC 632/.754—dc23
LC record available at https://lccn.loc.gov/2019045792

A stink bug spent the winter
in the hollow of an oak tree
with some other stink bugs.

Another stink bug spent the winter in leaves under an oak tree. One warm day in May, the stink bugs crawled out.

They flew around in the warm air. One made a stink.
The other liked it.

They got together and mated.

JUNE 8

This is when my story began. I was one of the twenty-eight eggs laid on the underside of this leaf.

JUNE 13

I hatched today.

"Hooray!" said nobody but me.

JUNE 29

There were some really good things to eat here!

But why did everyone keep saying, "Ew. Stink bug!"?
I don't think I smell so bad.

JULY 4

I was minding my own business eating some lettuce
when a bird tried to eat me. I stunk him. He spat me out.

16

It was a good day to *molt*—shed
my skin. This is my third molt.

I wriggled out of my old skin

so I could grow some more.
I don't have real wings yet,
so I can't fly.

JULY 15

I had my proboscis (the thing I use to suck food) in a tomato when a grasshopper came by, all bossy, and knocked me over.

STINK! I let him have it.

AUGUST 10

Five molts and I was fully grown. Look at me!
I had real wings and I could fly!

"Hooray!" said nobody but me.

23

AUGUST 12

I flew around some more. Jackpot! This farm
had all of my favorites. Apples, peppers, peaches.
I couldn't decide what to eat first.

AUGUST 14

This pepper looked good. I stuck my proboscis in it for a while.

26

AUGUST 20

It was a little chilly tonight. Look at these peaches! Yum! *

AUGUST 27

I was having dinner in the cabbage patch when a skunk came by. What a STINK he made!

Thanks!

Here
I am

SEPTEMBER 2

A stink bug made a stink to meet in this cornfield.
Glad he did! Corn is delicious!

SEPTEMBER 14

A green bug flew by that looked and
smelled like me. I wonder if we're related.

SEPTEMBER 20

It was getting cold at night. I was looking for someplace on the ground to spend the winter when a mouse surprised me. I gave him a stink. It didn't bother him. I flew away just in time.

I'm down here

34

OCTOBER 1

I smelled another stink to meet on this dead, old tree. Lots of stink bugs were already here.

OCTOBER 7

I'll just squeeze under this bark and spend the winter here. See you next spring!

GLOSSARY

instar: a phase between two periods of molting

invasive species: a species that is not native to an area and that can cause harm to the environment, human health, or human economy

marmorated: veined or streaked like marble

molt: shed old feathers, hair, skin, or a shell to make way for new growth

proboscis: a body part that contains cutting blades and a two-channelled tube for feeding

SOURCES AND RECOMMENDED READING

Periodical
Kathryn Schulz. "When Twenty-Six Thousand Stinkbugs Invade Your Home." *The New Yorker.* March 12, 2018.

Websites
https://cisr.ucr.edu/
brown_marmorated_stinkbug.html

https://en.wikipedia.org/wiki/
Brown_marmorated_stink_bug

https://hortnews.extension.iastate.edu/
brown-marmorated-stink-bug

https://www.stopbmsb.org

* Though stink bugs are more likely to stay in one place and feed on one food, in this book S. Bug feeds on more than one food to show the wide range of a stink bug's taste.

A female stink bug will lay twenty to thirty eggs on the underside of a leaf. She will do this about once a week in the summer. That means one stink bug can lay more than two hundred eggs each summer. The nymphs hatch four or five days after being laid.

The nymphs have five life stages, or instars, in five weeks. They shed their skin and grow each time.

In about two months they are mature and have the shield that gives stink bugs their distinctive

TREES

THINGS STINK BUGS EAT

NUTS

FRUITS

VEGETABLES

CEREAL CROPS